ACCELERATE
YOUR
LEARNING

*Practical Strategies to Learn Faster,
Sharpen Memory, and Explode Your
Personal Expertise and Knowledge
in No Time*

Pollux Andrews

Table Of Contents:

Introduction

Why should you bother about accelerated learning? After all, just like most other human beings, you're constantly learning. In fact, every single day, we either learn something new or we supplement or enhance the things that we already know.

Why accelerate the process?

Well, please understand that when you accelerate how you pick up new information and, just as importantly, implement that information, you gain a competitive advantage. You save a tremendous amount of time, effort and, yes, money. How come?

Well, we are constantly asked to learn new materials for work. Make no mistake, if you work at a job where you are not expected to learn anything new, you have hit a dead end. At the very least, even if there is no formal skills training system at your place of work, if you take it upon yourself to learn to become more productive, efficient and effective, a lot of great things happen.

First, you're more likely to get promoted. Second, you're probably more likely to get a raise. Third, you might even qualify for enhanced training programs. In other words, you open up quite a number of opportunities for yourself by simply deciding to speed up your personal learning process.

Similarly, you learn new instructions as part of your daily life. I'm not just talking about work or productivity here. I'm talking about your relationships.

Also, from a purely personal perspective, we are curious about a wide range of topics. For example, whatever you read on a day to day basis, chances are, you're curious about certain topics. Wouldn't it be awesome if you were able to process more information so you can get the info that you need, whether it's for professional or personal reasons?

The compelling reason, as far as I'm concerned regarding the need for accelerated learning involves our modern world. Look around you, look at your workplace, look at your industry. You should notice that people who are rewarded the most and are considered the most authoritative and credible tend to be specialists.

They're not jacks of all trades. They're not walking encyclopedias that people from all over can talk to about everything under the sun. Instead, their knowledge tends to be a foot wide and ten miles deep.

Believe it or not, that kind of specialty is what the modern world rewards the most. There's a high demand for expert learning and rare knowledge.

Unfortunately, to get this level of expertise, you're going to have to process a tremendous amount of information. If you're not going to process these materials in a relatively workable amount of time, you're going to get left behind. You're going to suffer the consequences of opportunity costs.

Make no mistake, if you want to be more successful, you need to learn quickly and effectively. The modern global economy is a knowledge economy. Quick learning is crucial to any kind of success.

Even if you just wanted to stay in place, you still need to pick up the pace as far as your ability to learn goes. Otherwise, you run the very real risk of becoming obsolete.

If you need proof of this, just look at the hundreds of job categories that are quickly disappearing in the United States. We are already in the age of mobile devices. Next, we will enter the world of 3D printing and big data.

The pace of technology continues to speed up. Unfortunately, most people could barely keep up. In fact, in the case of too many people, they're still stuck in the internet age. That is at least two ages behind.

We went through the social media age, the mobile age, and now we're in the world of 3D printing, big data, artificial intelligence, machine learning. You have to keep up.

But there are **three key problems** that you're going to run into as you try to keep up with the change in the global economy.

Problem #1: Generally speaking, the human mind can only process so much information before it gets overloaded

I don't care how smart you are, I don't care how many degrees you have, I don't care how high your IQ is or what your past accomplishments are. Unless you figure out how to make accelerated learning for you, it's only a matter of time until you get overloaded and you feel burned out.

Problem #2: In the modern world, we are suffering from information overload, not information scarcity

Another key challenge you're facing is the fact that every single day, the amount of information humans can learn increases almost exponentially. Did you know that every single hour hundreds of thousands of photos are uploaded to Facebook? Did you know that every single day, over two million pieces of new content is published on the internet?

These statistics are mind boggling. That's how much information there is out there. How do you make sense of it? How do you turn learning or managing that information into some sort of system?

We have gone from a world where a lot of global knowledge can fit into a few libraries, to a place where you can now fit thousands of libraries in a flash drive. Guess what? The number of libraries that need to be stored keeps increasing on a day to day basis.

Problem #3: Most people simply don't have the time

Let me tell you, if you are anywhere like a typical American, chances are, you wish that there were more hours in a day. You are saddened by the fact that there are only 24 hours in any given day.

The truth is, regardless of how much time we have, we quickly figure a way to fill out our schedule. It seems like you don't really need to put in much effort. All sorts of duties, obligations and responsibilities pop up to fill up your schedule.

How can you improve your learning ability and information processing skills if you simply don't have the time? You need to navigate these three key problems for you to stay ahead of the curve.

Accelerated Learning is the Solution

Thankfully, accelerated learning is the solution to the three problems I have outlined above. Accelerated learning enables you to quickly learn the information you need to learn to take your knowledge to the next level.

Accelerated learning is not theory, nor is it speculation. You're not going to deal with hypothetical situations or theories or things that "would be nice" if they existed. Instead, accelerated learning uses concepts that have been tried and proven over the years.

Also, accelerated learning is a long term solution. It is not a hack, it is not a band-aid solution, it is not some sort of short term accommodation. It is the real deal. Get this right and you adopt a skill that will continue to benefit you many years from now.

Best of all, accelerated learning enables you to work with your schedule. Maybe you have 15 hours per day, maybe you have a couple of hours to spare, it doesn't matter. As long as you have time, you can master accelerated learning.

It doesn't matter how much time you have, as long as you're consistent in your efforts at picking up this skill, you will be okay.

Accordingly, this type of learning system is both flexible and versatile. It fits your personal lifestyle and circumstances.

You don't have to put your life on hold to learn this set of skills. You can pick it up incrementally, or you can schedule in a small chunk of training every single day. As long as you are consistent, you will benefit from it.

Finally, it's highly portable. Maybe this week you are going to be on the other side of the planet on a vacation. Maybe you're going blogging and going from city to city. Maybe you work part time jobs and you have an unusual shifting schedule. It doesn't matter. Accelerated learning is highly portable.

You don't have to go to some sort of physical brick and mortar center. You only need to read this book and learn the modules. It is something that becomes part of you if you let it.

Make no mistake, if you want to take your life to the next level and become a more effective person, you need to pick up accelerated learning skills.

Chapter 1: Why Do Most People Stop Learning in High School?

Make no mistake, learning habits are choices. Please read what I just said again. I did not say that learning is a choice. I'm saying, **learning habits** are choices.

The way you learn, whether good or bad, is a choice.

You have to wrap your mind around this fundamental fact. Otherwise, you're going to put yourself in the impossible situation of thinking that your learning ability is somehow set in stone.

I can't even begin to tell you how many people believe this. A lot of people will swear that they were born to learn at a certain rate. Do you see how discouraging that is?

It simply just reduces one's ability to learn to a case of a genetic lottery. If you have the right genes or the right physical background, you will be able to learn at optimal rates. Too bad if you do not win the genetic lottery and your parents are slow. So, by definition, you have to be slow too.

Thankfully, that's not the truth. The truth is, your learning habits, as debilitating or limiting as they may be right now, are choices. Since you chose to pick them up, you can choose to replace them. Do you see how this works?

Here's the problem. We stop picking up learning habits in high school. From that point on, too many of us assume that the way we learn is set in stone. We have adopted a certain learning track and we assume that these are inescapable.

This is not true. And it doesn't follow that you should stop in high school.

The Causes of a Premature End to Personal Learning

You have to understand that most people do not choose to stop learning in high school. While their learning habits are choices, they did not all of a sudden just wake up one day and decide to stop learning in new ways in high school. Instead, they fall into a pattern.

First of all, they develop habitual learning. In other words, we comprehend and incorporate new information based on existing learning strategies, skills and patterns.

Now, this might seem neutral, it might even seem natural, but here's the problem: your learning strategies, skills and learning patterns are choices.

At this point, we stopped choosing new patterns, skills and strategies. Instead, we rely on processes that we think already works for us. Put simply, we end up settling for cents on the dollar.

If your mind is capable of 100% production, you end up settling for a tiny fraction of that. This is due to habitual learning.

I can understand why this is so tempting to a lot of people. When you think habitually, it seems so easy. It seems so natural. It seems like your conclusions just flow.

But the problem is, you may be settling too early. Maybe with a little bit more challenge and a little bit more curiosity, you can come up with other learning habits that would adequately prepare you for a very challenging information economy landscape.

Another reason why people end their personal learning curve in high school is peer pressure. They hang out with people who have very low expectations or people who are just set in their ways and, for whatever reason, do not want to change.

You have to always remember that attitudes are infectious. As the old saying goes, birds of a feather flock together. If you want to know a person, look at his friends. That's how you know who he really is.

Peer pressure is real, and it is no surprise that people who think and learn at a certain level hang out together. If you need proof of this, think back to high school. Look at the kids that go on to be power lawyers, captains of industry – the big winners in life. They tend to hang out together.

On the other end of the spectrum are late starters, people who struggle for the rest of their lives, and people who can't seem to get it together. Guess what? They too hang out together.

Another reason why people stop learning in high school is simple lack of challenge. Let me tell you, right now, it's very easy to not challenge your brain while engaging.

What am I talking about? Well, as recently as ten years ago, if you wanted a mental challenge, you'd pick up a book, read classic literature, or play a board game. The social interaction of those games, as well as the classical analysis of the human condition contained in literature, challenges your brain.

You have to understand that your mind is like a muscle. Just like a muscle, if you put pressure and stress on it, it gets bigger, stronger, and is able to endure. On the other hand, if you barely challenge it, it becomes soft, weak, and is unable to handle much pressure. You give up quickly.

If you need proof of this, look at kids who play video games all day. Look at people who look at their mobile devices all day.

They have short attention spans, they are very impatient, and it's very hard for them to put in the time, effort and energy to pick up new information. This is due to the fact that people don't challenge themselves intellectually as much as before.

A lot of this has to do with the popularity of mobile devices like tablets and mobile phones, video game consoles, and what have you. These activities tend to distract from mental activities that require more effort like reading.

It is not a surprise that too many people no longer pick up physical books. Instead, they'd rather watch a video on their mobile device or play a game. This leads to another set of behaviors that reduce the amount of mental challenges you give yourself on a day to day basis. People tend to engage in non-challenging discussions like gossip.

Also, thanks to social media, it's not unusual for people to like or "friend" people online who share the same political or social views as them. What happens is that **you end up in an echo chamber.**

When you like or share any kind of content, chances are, the people on your friend list share the same information. So you're basically just bouncing the same type of info to each other. Nobody's really growing because you're not presented with an opposing view.

When you come across somebody who has a totally different opinion than you, you are given the opportunity to back up your opinion. You're given the opportunity to explain why you believe what you believe.

Finally, given the developments above, it is no surprise that we live in a world where negative attitudes towards deep thinking and analysis are all too common. In fact, a lot of people are saying, "Why do I need to step up my learning rate? After all, if it ain't broke, why fix it?"

Well, here's the problem, a little bit of inefficiency at the beginning grows over time. It scales up. It gets worse and worse because it gets plugged into your mental habits. The less you challenge yourself, the harder it would be to break out of these mental habits.

But You're Still Learning New Stuff, Right?

Sure, to mature as an adult, you still have to learn new materials. You learn things at work, you learn things about other people, your social interactions, and your relationships. But the problem is, unless you address the issues above and you get out from under your negative mental habits, you're going to learn in a very inefficient way. As I've mentioned above, this inefficiency scales up over time.

The Inefficiency Gap

As you get older, to become an expert, you need to learn more concepts and pick up more data and process them. You should already know this. In fact, most people understand this.

But the problem is, as they get older, the more inefficient they become. Like I said, the mental inefficiencies scales up over time. You can still learn new things, but your uptake declines.

How do you think your mind responds? Very simple. You end up feeling stressed, overburdened, and needing more time to produce.

It is not an accident that as more Americans put in more time at work, they're actually not improving their productivity as much as you would expect. Put in another way, people are putting in the time, but getting less out of the time they put in.

This has nothing to do with being lazy, okay? Let's get that out of the way. Nor does this have anything to do with being dumb. Instead, it's all about efficiency.

Because the effort is all too real. People are stressed out, overburdened, and are on the brink of burn out. That cannot be denied.

But the problem is, since they did not address this internal learning efficiency issue, they need more and more time to produce. Eventually, things bog down so badly that they need more and more time to produce the same amount as before.

Chapter 2: Key Challenges in Effective Learning

I hope that by reading Chapter 1, you now have a clear understanding of why you need to adopt accelerated learning skills. I hope we're on the same page.

Well, if you're pumped up and excited about increasing your learning efficiency, please understand that you are facing 5 key challenges. That's right, people looking to boost their ability to learn face **5 key challenges**. You have to overcome all of these to master accelerated learning.

1. Attitude

Let's face it, there's a lot of truth to the old saying, "You can't teach an old dog new tricks." It's not because people are substantially dumber when they get older. In fact, people in their fifties make way more money than when they were in their twenties. They are rewarded by society in the form of positions of authority.

This is not a question of a failure to learn. Instead, it's a question of attitude. **Because when you get older, it's easy to think that you have learned what you need to learn**. It's easy to think in terms of shorthand.

For example, how many times have you come across somebody who says, "I've seen that before" or "If you've seen one, you've seen it all." This is called "**associative analysis**." In other words, when you get older, you start looking for patterns.

You're no longer looking to understand things in terms of basic principles or basic elements. It's not like you're a high school or college student again where you're learning new concepts and you're just poking around and assembling and disassembling new concepts until they make sense to you.

Instead, as an older person, you look at new things and see how they line up with the things that you already know. And if you see certain similarities, you assume that they are similar enough to what you already know, and you make decisions on them.

Now, don't get me wrong. For the most part, this works. This is part of the reason why older people tend to make more money. They're more authoritative and credible.

But, as I've mentioned earlier, we live in a post-information age economy. Simply making associations with stuff that you already know is simply not going to cut it anymore. You're going to have to learn new stuff completely. I'm talking about brand new concepts like blockchain or 3D printing or big data.

Another attitude that you need to watch out for is the thinking "I can't change how my mind works." This is really a cop out. Nobody's asking you to completely rewire your mind.

Instead of some sort of hardware modification, accelerated learning is all about working with your habits so they work for you instead of against you. You're not being asked to download a new brain. Unfortunately, if your attitude is "I can't change how my mind works," you are basically closing the door to any possibility of improvement.

You have to understand that your attitude may be getting in the way. Once you become aware of that, then it becomes easier for you to choose to believe in other assumptions that can make accelerated learning happen.

2. Time

If you keep telling yourself, "I'm just too busy for this kind of stuff," guess what will happen? That's right, you will be too busy. When you keep saying to yourself that you really don't have the time, you are closing the door of opportunity to learning what you need to learn to take your life to the next level.

Instead of thinking that you're too busy, think about what you stand to lose. Instead of saying, "I'm too busy for this kind of stuff," why not think, "I can't afford to miss this kind of stuff." Focus on what you stand to lose.

I understand that time is money, but please understand that the value of your time will increase tremendously if you adopt the right learning skills.

3. Lack of information

Another set of challenges that you're going to have to overcome involves your attitude regarding information. In particular, your lack of information about accelerated learning. Even if you are completely on board regarding your need to adopt this skill set, it's very easy to let certain attitudes regarding lack of information to prevent you from learning what you need to learn.

For example, if you think that it just takes too much effort to figure out where to start, that's going to be a problem. Also, if you keep insisting that there has to be some sort of stripped down, easy to understand "cheat sheet" that you only need to read once, this could be a problem. You have to overcome these attitudes.

Understand that mastering accelerated learning requires an investment, not only of time, effort and energy, but also focus.

Again, you don't have to learn it all at once. You don't have to do it in one sitting, but you have to be committed to learning it. This is why the mindset of some of "learning shortcut" can undermine your ability to pick up this skill.

Now, please understand that accelerated learning is a learning skill. If you are able to master this, you will be able to speed up the rate in which you appreciate and incorporate new information.

4. Distractions

The fourth set of challenges that you're going to have to deal with involves distractions. Look at your current lifestyle. Do you engage in certain activities that soak up your attention? These are leisure activities like spending a lot of time staring into a small screen or some other gadget. This can also involve sitting on a couch for hours on and playing video games.

The problem with these activities is, they take up a lot of focus. The more you engage in these activities, the shorter your attention span becomes. The same process applies to consuming internet content. Do you notice that when you scan your Facebook timeline, you're not really reading? You're just scanning for certain keywords.

If you see a picture or you see a video automatically start to play that attracts your attention, that's when you stop. But other than that, you're just scanning. It's no surprise that people scroll really fast. It is a minor miracle that they are able to make sense of any of that stuff because they're scrolling so fast. They just have so much information to get through.

Well, you have to understand the effect of all of these factors on your ability to learn. You're going to have to overcome video game and gadget addiction, so you can free up enough focus and willpower to pick up accelerated learning.

5. Impatience

Let's get one thing clear. Our modern world has essentially trained us to be impatient. Gone are the days where you have to wait for a significant amount of time to get stuff delivered, get stuff done, or otherwise see certain results in your life. Now, people want pizza to be delivered not in an hour or half an hour, but in 15 minutes, otherwise, they expect it to be free.

Similarly, if you buy stuff on the internet, you'd like the product delivered, if not the next day, the day after. It seems that our decreasing attention span is dictating our expectations about our material world. We have developed this mindset of "get to the good stuff ASAP!"

This impatience sabotages your ability to put in the time, effort and energy to master accelerated learning. It really does. You feel that things have to happen instantly. It doesn't work that way. While accelerated learning can turbocharge your ability to pick up new information and dramatically shorten your learning curve, it requires some patience to learn.

It's not some sort of magical pill that you take and all of a sudden, you add 40 points to your IQ.

I'm sure that you must be facing some of the challenges as stated above. In fact, most people don't get motivated enough to master the accelerated learning skills due to these challenges only. However, if you want to grow faster in any area of life, you need to learn new things every day, be it a new skill, new program, new language, or new approaches of getting things done.

Next chapter will explain how accelerated learning skills will help you to pace up your voyage of learning anything new and thereafter you will learn seven key elements of accelerated learning.

Chapter 3: Accelerated Learning- A Practical Approach

Accelerated learning is a series of skills that stack up. That's all it is. It's a set of skills that you are going to learn in that when you learn them one by one, they reinforce each other. They stack up over time. In other words, if you master on skill and then you follow it up with another skill, the previous skill increases and enhances the value of subsequent skills.

The more skills you stack up, the faster you learn. Things get easier and easier as you practice each and every skill set you adopt. As a result, your overall ability to appreciate, comprehend and incorporate information scales up over time. Now, don't get too excited.

In the beginning, since you are working on the first skill set, you're going to face quite a bit of a resistance. This is natural. After all, you haven't done this before. You're just getting accustomed to learning in a different way. But after you have learned one skill set after another, things become easier.

You are able to connect the dots, you are not as intimidated as before, and it's not uncommon for things to become habitual. Finally, you know you have reached a totally different level when all these skill sets have become a part of you. They no longer feel like some sort of foreign or external hack or band aid solution. You no longer feel like you're going through some sort of checklist.

Instead, this is something that you feel comes out of you naturally. Once you reach that point, you have essentially reconfigured not only your attitude, but your internal coping processes to the whole concept of learning.

Seven Elements Of Accelerated Learning

After this chapter, I'm going to go through an in-depth discussion of each of the seven elements of accelerated learning (as listed below). I'm also going to include scientific studies that back up many of these components. In this chapter, I'm just going to give you an overview of the seven key elements that constitute practical accelerated learning.

Please understand that this book places special emphasis on the word "practical." There is no shortage of books on accelerated learning as a theory. I'm sure that's not what you're looking for. You are looking to get hired for the right job. You are looking to get promoted. You are looking for a pay raise. You are looking to become more persuasive.

In other words, you are looking for practical results. This is why this book is written in practical terms. There are just so many things to talk about, but we focus instead on the bare minimum we need to set up and maintain and personal accelerated learning system that works.

Keep that in mind. If you read other accelerated learning books, they would focus on different elements, they would have a lot more moving parts, but my number one focus with this book is to give you a practical approach to accelerated learning.

The seven key elements of accelerated learning are:

1. Bite-sized learning

2. Association learning

3. Power of visualization in mastering new concepts

4. Sensory learning

5. Connecting the dots quick breaks

6. Memory incorporation

7. Keep challenging yourself by scaling and leveling up

Each of these elements has different practices, so it's really important to zero in on the concept as a whole and then look at how they're actually carried out in practical terms. Do each of these elements until you feel comfortable with them. Keep doing them and practicing them until you can do them automatically.

Once you are able to do that, move on to the next element. However, if you still feel that a specific element is challenging or it takes you quite a while to get going, keep at it. This is not a race. Don't think that you need to adopt each and every piece in rapid succession. You're missing the point if you do that.

Instead, you're shooting for mastery because, like I said in a previous chapter, when you adopt a skill set, it scales up and reinforces the next skill set. But to make things easy on yourself, you have to set this up right. That's why you have to first master each and every element.

The good news is, as you go along, it becomes easier and easier to master each subsequent element because you are reinforcing them with skills that you've learned before.

Chapter 4: Use Chunk Learning To Retain Better and Longer

I cannot forget my first week in college. I was very excited about being hundreds of miles away from my parents in this college town, but my excitement went up in flames when the professor for one of my classes handed out a syllabus along with the reading list. The reading list was not optional. There was a timeline with the reading list.

As I looked through the required reading, I was supposed to essentially read 50,000 words every single week. This was a serious problem for me because I could barely get myself to read a 200-page book in two months. I obviously had to change my attitude towards learning, otherwise there was a big danger that I might flunk out.

50,000 words translates to around 200 pages every single week. Now, I thought this was the extent of my problems. But then I went to the next class and it's the same thing. The syllabus required me to read 50,000 words. When I've gotten all the reading lists for all the courses I signed up for, I was expected to read somewhere north of 300,000 words per week or 10 days. Talk about a baptism by fire.

I wished I had learned the power of learning in chunks back then. Unfortunately, I thought that the only way to deal with all that reading it to basically just power through them, total immersion. I would basically go to a café several blocks away from the dorms where I was staying and just camp out in 8-hour blocks.

I set up my schedule in such a way that I only had to go to school Monday, Wednesday and Friday. For the rest of the week, I sat in a corner of that café with a huge stack of books in front of me. Miraculously, I was able to read through all that stuff. But let me tell you, it wasn't pleasant. I felt like I was forcefeeding my brain.

It was no surprise that when the time came for me to write essays based on what I read, I didn't do all that well. My problem was, I was cramming too much with no framework or organizing principle in a very restricted amount of time. If I had only learned about the power of bite-sized learning, I probably would have gotten much better grades.

The truth is, when we learn new concepts as a whole, it's very easy for our brains to suffer from data overload. Not surprisingly, if you read a book and you aren't smart about it by cross referencing what you learned with cliff's notes or some other summary reference, you end up with a very common problem. You end up being unable to tell the forest from the trees.

At the end of that process of reading all those materials, you feel overstressed, intimidated and discouraged. It is no surprise that a lot of my friends who had to deal with the same amount of volume reading felt that they can only process so much. In fact, a lot of them dropped classes and had to take repeat classes.

A few of them did this so often that they added several years to their college careers. I know one guy who took a total of 11 years to finish college. Crazy, right? Well, if you choose to learn in chunks, you don't have to do that.

A Step By Step Guide To Bite-Sized Learning

Follow these steps to accelerate your ability to learn by learning in small chunks

Step #1 : Understand the overview concept

Look at the concept that you're trying to learn. In other words, think along the lines of "this is what we do because of..." or "this thing works like this because of..." You can apply the same to books, "this book is about..." What is the big concept? What is the big lesson? What is the big truth the book brings to the table?

Regardless of what you're reading, everything can be broken down into some sort of concept. You don't have to have a crystal clear view of it at this point in time, but you just have to have a rough understanding of what the overview concept is.

Tie the overview of what with why

When you ask yourself why you are supposed to learn this stuff, usually in a college reading list, the professor would have themes tied to each book. For example, if you are supposed to read the autobiography of Malcolm X or certain parts of the Quran and the confessions of St. Augustine, the overview might be personal revelation.

What is it about personal revelation that relates to the word why? Well, it can involve storytelling, the ability to communicate and key fundamental truths about the human condition that transcends cultures and geographic barriers. Think in these broad terms. Tie the overview of what you're supposed to learn with why you're supposed to learn it.

Benefit from purpose-driven understanding

If you're able to do the two things above, **you develop purpose-driven understanding**. You're not just reading this material randomly. You're not just taking shots in the dark and settling for whatever you get. There is reason why you're doing things. Now, it doesn't have to be crystal clear, but at least it's much better than just totally being in the dark.

This reduces the chances of you being confused quite a bit.

Step # 2: Go from big concepts to parts

In this step, you're going to learn how specific operations one by one, or in the case of literature, specific themes, one by one. If you're trying to master scientific information, medical concepts or legal concepts, focus on each concept and how it ties to a larger concept. For example, in law, jurisdiction is a big concept, but it's tied into the even larger category of legal procedure.

Think in terms of concepts being broken down into smaller and smaller parts and get a clear understanding of the specific operations of each of these smaller parts. When you do this, you are going from the big overview downwards and then back to the big overview and eventually, you tie it to the purpose behind why you're trying to understand the big concept in the first place.

For example, if you're a law student and you're trying to learn the concept of personal jurisdiction, that ties into the concept of legal procedure. Under the American Constitutional Law, you can't just drag people into a State Court randomly. It doesn't work that way. There is this concept of personal jurisdiction, but this is tied to the larger concept of procedure.

What is the right procedure and what is the purpose behind that procedure? Usually, these purposes are to avoid unfairness, which is tied to surprise. For example, if I live in Utah, it would surprise me if a plaintiff is able to drag me into court in Florida. The procedure must be set up in such a way that there is no surprise and this ties into the even larger purpose of fairness.

Do you see how this works? You can apply this analysis to anything; medical concepts, new processes that you have to learn at work, even understanding your partner and your relationship. There are just so many things that you can apply this to. The key is to go from the big concepts to the parts. Learn each specific operation one by one, tie them to your overview of how things work and then tie this to a larger purpose.

If you are able to do this, eventually, you learn all the parts and fit them all together. The good thing about this is that you're not putting yourself in a position to learn everything all at once. You're not mastering everything in one sitting because that's going to prove to be too much to your system.

Sure, a lot of people can do this. I have no doubt about that. But they're running a very high risk of data overload. You don't want to burn out.

Step #3: Keep repeating

Make no mistake, the first time you figure this stuff out, it's as if scales fell off your eyes. It's easy to get excited. But the thing is, this is not going to benefit you all that much unless you keep repeating it day in and day out. The more you repeat it, the more its effectiveness scales up and the less emotionally intimidated you become.

Accordingly, you should take advantage of all opportunities to repeat the steps above. Apply them to as many different situations you see.

In a 2013 study out of the University of Sheffield, two groups of study participants consisting of students and teachers were observed. One group focused on teaching and the other focused on research. When the students were given small questionnaires during the sessions, they reported that this small of bite-sized information gathering was helpful in helping them pick up new skills.

Interestingly enough, when the teaching sessions revolved around these small questionnaires and the sessions were fairly short, questionnaire results indicate that these students were able to learn in 20 minutes. This highlights the power of learning in bite-sized chunks.

In a study out of North Carolina State University published in 2012, 22 students were observed regarding their ability to master scientific concepts involving agricultural biotechnology. This material is notoriously complicated and hard to understand. The study showed that when the curriculum was focused on contextual teaching and was geared to prevent overload, the students were able to learn better.

In another 2013 Kent State University study, 64 students were observed for certain learning techniques; mnemonics, rereading, using images to learn text and other approaches. It turned out that when they used these techniques in modules, they were able to achieve greater results as far as their ability to absorb and use information.

All these studies prove nothing but the effective of bite-sizing the learning material and thus improving the absorption and retention of information in your brain. And the 3-step process is the way to get started.

Chapter 5: Effective Fusion of Old and New Concepts & Explode Learning

Now that you know the overview and component parts of a new idea, you have to tie them to the past. In other words, since you already know about what happened in the past and you already have an opinion about things that you are aware of from the past, you can layer new information onto old information.

This is a very important part of accelerated learning. If you are just going to hang on to new information you picked up in some sort of mental vacuum, it's very easy to forget those concepts. Ask yourself, what concepts do I already know that seem similar enough to the new things I'm trying to learn? How are these different? How do they vary in a significant way? Which situations do these two sets of information apply to?

When you come up with practical answers to these, you will be able to not only use your existing knowledge as a platform for new information, but you would also be able to separate new information from old information. You would be able to know where your old understanding stops and the new concepts you just learned begin.

In fact, our brains are not designed to recall information in isolation; instead, we group information together into one associative memory. The associated learning works on the principle that ideas reinforce each other and can be linked to one another. That's why it is difficult to recall just one eyebrow without seeing the whole face.

It's really important to understand application. Often times, this is what separates the stuff that we know already from the information that we're trying to learn. It also helps when you are able to mentally categorize concepts you already know and concepts you are learning. The more you can keep these apart, the more you will be able to compare and contrast them both in terms of content and application.

Keep repeating

It's really important to keep repeating this process of associating new concepts to the stuff that you already know. Take advantage of all the other opportunities that present themselves to repeat your actions. Be on the lookout for new information and try to mentally connect this to existing knowledge.

In a 2014 University of Minnesota Medical School experiment, 20 children were observed from birth to preschool. The researchers found that when these kids entered a new phase in their development, they would engage in behavior that is tried and proven. For example, the researchers put a toy on top of a table. Test subjects would shake the table to bring the toy down.

At that age, they could have easily used a stick or they could have climbed the chair next to the table. Still, they preferred shaking the table because this worked with other things in the past. This worked in previous situation. Even though they found themselves in a new situation with a new toy, they applied the old method.

In other words, they applied new concept and new situations to things that they already know. These are practices that, to them, are tried and proven.

In a 2013 research study by Erica Wojcik out of the University of Wisconsin, Madison, 23 kids were observed in terms of their ability to learn new words. This study involved infants that could not speak yet, but they were exposed to new words. The study showed that pre-verbal children are able to remember new words by associating it or integrating it with their early memories.

Infants can actually hang on to a new word over a very long period of time. The experiment used labels and things that refer to these labels to test if these kids actually picked up a new word and remembered previous words. By simply associating things that they just learned with previous knowledge, they are able to pick up quite a lot of new information.

Charlie Munger, long-time partner of Warren Buffett also recommends that you have to learn multiple concepts from different disciplines; but you have to combine the learning from all these different principle and prepare latticework of different concepts. This association of different concepts forces you to apply the old learned principles in to new learning or modify your previous understanding of concept based on the new things you learn. Learning without association is like storing knowledge of different subjects in separate compartments; and you really can't learn holistically with this approach and it takes much longer time.

Chapter 6: Harness Mental Imagery to Master New Concepts

By this point, you already know how to break new concepts down into smaller, more chewable and easier to understand parts. You have also learned how to associate the new concepts to things that you already know.

When you break down new ideas into smaller parts, many of those parts are actually not new at all. In fact, either they are completely already in your memory banks or a large part of each piece is already familiar to you. Whatever the case, you're not dealing with something completely new, foreign, and yes, intimidating.

This is why when you associate these new concepts or parts of new concepts to the things you already know, it becomes easier for you to understand them and remember them. You're also able to understand where these concepts apply and where they do not apply. Of course, the more you repeat this, the clearer things become.

But here is the thing. **You can take things to a whole other level by using visualization to aid the process**. Please understand that you can achieve a tremendous amount of progress just doing the first two steps of accelerated learning. But if you apply visualization, it's like pouring gas onto hot coals. You're going to get a lot more things done in a shorter period of time.

How come? Our minds think in terms of big picture concepts. We tend to use sensory reference points when thinking about or processing ideas. This is why this is a big deal.

When I say visualize, I'm not just talking about your ability to see. I'm not just referring to your ability to look at some sort of big picture or some sort of vista or landscape in front of you. **By "visualization," I'm talking in broad terms regarding your five senses.**

Some people visualize by hearing. In fact, according to studies, women are more **auditory** or listening-based in their visualization, and men tend to be **optical**

based. They tend to focus on what they can see.

But these are broad generalizations. If you break this down, some people "visualize" through the **sense of smell**. In fact, certain studies indicate that olfactory memories are more reliable. When we associate a memory with a certain smell, it sticks with us for a far longer period of time.

Some people visualize things by the **sense of touch**. These are tactile people.

Finally, some other individuals are **taste oriented**. They visualize or organize certain concepts based on an experience involving them eating or drinking something.

Please understand that there are no right or wrong answers here. What's important is that you are able to zero in and take advantage of your mind's preferred visualization mode.

If you prefer to see things, fine. If you are more partial to the things that you hear, great. If you prefer remembering or making sense of things based on your sense of smell, wonderful. If you prefer touch, no problem. If you prefer taste, that's great too. It doesn't really matter.

What matters is you tie in new concepts or parts of new concepts to your sensory capabilities. This enables you to not only remember things better, but to also engage with these concepts.

They're no longer free floating out there. They are no longer theory. They are no longer things that you have to learn, like stuff that your college or high school professor spits out. They're not outside of you.

In this context, your senses act as some sort of gateway or bridge between the information that is otherwise free floating, and your internal ability to make sense of things. Here are the steps that you can follow.

Now, please understand that everybody's different, just as we all have different sensory preferences. Feel free to mix and match or make necessary adjustments to fit your set of circumstances as well as your personal preferences.

Visualize the Concept's Problem or Context

The first thing that you need to do is to use your senses to visualize the problem behind the concept.

For example, you work for an insurance company and your trainer introduced you to the idea of subrogation where any payouts made by your company to your insured client is going to be demanded from the other party's insurance company. To a lot of people, this is a very tricky, slippery, and otherwise complicated topic.

You have to visualize the problem first. What is the problem here? The problem, of course, is that your insurance company is paying the money up front.

Since your insured client is not at fault, it wouldn't be fair for them to take the hit because if they take the hit, your insurance premiums are going to go up. Pretty straightforward, right? So, out of fairness, they have to get it from the responsible party and their insurance company.

Now, you have to come up with some sort of visualization for that problem. The problem is fairness. The problem is: "where is the money going to come from?"

Maybe you'd have a diagram in your head. Maybe you'd have a short movie of Peter paying Mary, and then collecting from Paul. Whatever the case may be, come up with all sorts of easy to understand and easy to remember sensory signals.

Maybe you can imagine hearing in one ear the customer saying. "Where's my money?" and then hearing from the other ear the other insurance company's representative, "We've got you covered."

Regardless of how you make sense of this, you have to make sense of it using your senses because it makes it so much easier to remember and understand.

Visualize How the Idea Fits the Context

Now that you have an understanding that there is a problem here and you've visualized how the problem plays out, then play a mental movie or some sort of soundtrack, or maybe imagine yourself shaking hands or patting backs or engaging in other tactile experiences where the idea is solving the problem.

So in this case, imagine yourself on the phone, listening to the other insurance company, and you demanding that they pay your company the amount of money that you paid your insurance clients, otherwise, you're going to place another call to the legal department of your insurance company so they can sue the other company. It is probably a good idea to keep repeating the word "subrogation."

Similarly, you can visualize a nice flow chart of money or dollar signs flowing first from your company, and then flowing from another company back to your company. Regardless of how you do it, your visualization must let the idea fit the context or the problem.

In the first step, you visualize the problem. What is the problem that the idea is solving? And then you break down how the idea operates to solve problems or explain a situation or make a prediction.

Come Up with a Mental Movie

Even if you are not a very visual person, it does make sense to tie everything together in the form of a movie. Maybe you are an auditory person. You like to hear things. But you can easily apply that soundtrack to a movie of you being front and center dealing with the idea, coping with the problem, and making things happen.

It doesn't have to be long. It doesn't have to be overly complicated or dramatic. You can use very fast mental clips. They can be very short. Regardless, as long as they give you a big picture view of the problem, the solution, the internal mechanics of the problem, how things work, what is predicted, what can happen and how to resolve things, you would be okay.

Associate the Concept with Certain Sounds

Another shortcut you could use involves certain sounds, for example, the phone ringing or the word being pronounced.

For example, if somebody says "subrogation," you should have three key ideas pop up in your head immediately. Obviously, these things should have something to do with the problem subrogation solves, how subrogation works, and the steps needed to get a subrogation claim processed.

Associate the Concept with Body Movements

As I have mentioned above, you can pretend that you're patting peoples' backs or shaking people's hands to get a subrogation deal going.

Another example is, if you are a law student taking a class on evidence, you probably would struggle with the concept of hearsay. If you read a newspaper involving any kind of legal procedure and litigation, often times, the concept of hearsay is brought up. This is especially true when people are making accusations and filing charges.

Hearsay is not really a complicated legal concept. It's just easily misunderstood. It is an out of court statement offered in court to prove the truth of the matter asserted in the statement.

In other words, if Joe told me ten years ago far away that Mary is guilty of a certain crime, and then somebody took my statement and presented it in court and I'm not there, that is hearsay. It can get quite convoluted because there is hearsay through documents, there is hearsay through a chain of people talking to each other.

The concept of hearsay, along with the rule against perpetuities, have tripped up law students since time immemorial. It's a very easy concept to misunderstand. You can easily fix this problem by associating the concept with body movements.

You reach out with your left hand and say, "This is an out of court statement," and then you take out the other hand and you say, "Offered in court to prove the truth of the matter of the statement." And then you put your hands together and say, "This is hearsay."

And you keep repeating that and you realize that there are actually two major components of the concept. If any of these components are missing or their subparts, for example, it is not offered in court and it is not offered to prove the truth of the matter stated, then you don't have hearsay.

For instance, in my example above, if the person making the claim somehow subpoenas me and I show up at the court and I tell them what I know, what I know is hearsay. But when they subpoena the guy who told me, or they subpoenaed an actual party to the claim, then that won't be hearsay. That would be an admission.

I hope you can see how this all fits the manual breakdown of the otherwise easy to misunderstand concept of hearsay. It's no longer an out of court statement. You have the person who made the original claim out of court in front of you. You can cross examine him. It's an admission.

In a 2014 Ohio University study, 29 volunteers had their arms put in casts for a month. After the four weeks were over, the casts were taken off.

15 of the 29 didn't have to do anything. The other 14, during the four weeks, were asked to imagine themselves exercising the arm that was in the cast. They imagined themselves flexing, moving their wrists, and otherwise giving their arms a nice workout. Remember, their arms were in a cast from elbow to finger.

When the casts came off, it turned out that the people who did not do any arm exercises lost 45% of their arm strength. On the other hand, the ones who were doing visualization exercises only lost 25% arm strength.

This study by Brian Clark highlights the importance of visualization because it does have a physical outcome. What you choose to think about actually has a physical effect. It doesn't just stay in your mind. Accordingly, if you focus on breaking down ideas, you are able to carry out and engage with those ideas as you execute them in the real world involving physical actions or actual decisions.

In a 1996 University of Chicago study, there were three groups of study participants. The first group was asked to practice basketball for one hour every day. Another group was asked to just imagine themselves playing basketball. They're not asked to physically play basketball. The third group was not asked to do anything at all.

After 30 days have passed, each group was tested for their ability to shoot free throws. Each group's free throw accuracy was tested before and after the experiment.

Interestingly enough, after the 30 days were up, the group which practiced daily increased their free throw accuracy by 24%. They were making 24% more baskets. The ones who were just asked to visualize improved their free throw accuracy by 23%. The third group, which is the control group, showed no improvement.

This study, although it's fairly small, is very revealing regarding the power of visualization. It has a strong impact on actual physical performance. Similarly, when you are able to visualize concepts, you are able to absorb them to such an extent that your application of them can produce marked improvements when you carry them out.

Chapter 7: Life-Long Retention: How Mnemonics Works So Well

Mnemonics involve phrases, acronyms or sounds that are supposed to remind you of the concept you are trying to remember or implement. The ability to come up with mnemonics really boils down to a variation of the ability to connect the dots. In other words, you are tying stuff you're willing to know to the stuff you already know.

In Chapter 5, I went over this. Well, in this chapter, you're going to actually associate that process with certain words, certain sounds or certain images.

Maybe you can tie concepts to letters or you can tie words to letters. Regardless, you are engaged in the same thing. You're trying to tie stuff that you already know to stuff you want to know.

Common Mnemonics

This stuff is not new, so it's not like you're going to have to come up with something radically novel. Just do what people have been doing for a long time. People in school, whether in high school, college, graduate school, trade school, or vocational school, have been using mnemonics for a very long time.

You can use first letters of each concept. For example, according to American federal rules of evidence, you cannot use a defendant's character or past pattern of actions against that person. For example, if somebody is on trial for burglary that happened in September, you're not allowed to use the fact that this person has a record of breaking into houses for the past fifty years. However, there is an exception called the MIMIC exception.

This is a classic case of a mnemonic acronym. MIMIC stands for **motive, intent, mistake, identity or common scheme** or plan. Although it's inadmissible as part of US federal rules of evidence to introduce information from this person's past, if you notice that this person always has the same method, in other words, he or she has a common scheme or plan, that can be introduced. That will not be excluded by character evidence rules.

This can also apply for advice. For example, there are many highly poisonous marine snakes. Sometimes they find themselves on land.

You have to understand that these snakes have really powerful venom because catching fish in water is not easy. Fish are very slippery. They can also be very fast. It would help the snake tremendously if its venom almost instantly kills the fish it's trying to catch. This is why marine snakes that end up on land that bite people are extremely dangerous.

Throughout the years, people have come up with all sorts of mnemonics to capture life saving advice in a very easy to remember format. And one of these mnemonics is: *"Red touch yellow kills a fellow. Red touch black, friend of Jack."*

In other words, you look at the pattern of the coloring of the snake. If you notice that the snake has alternating bands of red, yellow and black, and the red touches the yellow part, it's a good idea to avoid that snake.

It's generally a good idea to avoid snakes. Period. But if you did get bit, there is at least some comfort in the fact that if red touched black. In other words, the snake is non-venomous. This is a good storytelling mnemonic for advice.

Another way you can master mnemonics is when you anchor the first letter of the concept's words to movie plots, characters or cartoons. What's so great about this mnemonic memorization technique is you don't just memorize the concept's parts. You also memorize the context: what it is used for, when do you use it, what needs to happen for the concept to even apply.

Keep repeating these, not just when you're sitting down and thinking about things or when you have time. Keep repeating this by taking advantage of all opportunities to repeat your actions. For example, if you see a book or YouTube videos of marine snakes, apply the mnemonic. The more you repeat these mnemonics in whatever form they take, the more likely you are going to remember them.

In a 2007 study out of the University of Illinois, 86 study participants were monitored by lead researcher Susan Goldman. The 86 participants were split up into two groups and studied. The first group involves fifth graders summarizing a children's story.

The interesting thing about the first group making summaries of the stories they heard was that these stories had song-like elements. The stories were mentioned with very engaging verbal sounds. And then the second group involved two versions of the story. One is less verbal or less sound oriented, and the other one more so.

The study was trying to determine what the effect of intonation or speech patterns may have on kids being able to remember concepts. It turns out that the first study, as well as the study in the second group, highlights the importance of intonation.

Students were able to remember stories told in an auditorily engaging way. In other words, they are able to recall the story. And when they were asked to tell the story, they were able to produce a higher quality retelling of the story.

This relates to mnemonics because we remember things based on our senses. And certain elements of the story were related in such a way that their auditory components left an imprint. Although each individual in the study remembers in a slightly different way, they all produced the result that intonation and delivery plays a major role in both remembrance as well as retelling quality.

This highlights the power of mnemonics because mnemonics are intended to increase retelling quality. It's not enough that you just remember. You're also able to retell the concept or the story at a high level of accuracy.

In a study published in 2014 out of Jagiellonian University in Krakow, Poland, 479 students were given a survey. They were asked basic demographic information as well as their use of mnemonics.

94% of the people taking the survey did not know what a mnemonic was. The remaining

6% knew what mnemonics were, but only 4% actually used these memory jogging and implementation boosting mental tools.

Interestingly enough, that same 4% segment of the participants had better grades compared to all the other students. This highlights the point that mnemonics do work. They were able to make sense of concepts and remember them better.

Chapter 8: Take More Breaks and Learn Faster

Let's get one thing clear, data overload is no joke. It is a serious problem. When you try to take in so many things and you are multitasking, you are flirting with burnout, if not breakdown. Your mind, after all, can only handle so much.

The problem with most people is that they think that they have to learn in one sitting, or they have to learn everything in one big chunk, or they only have this one block of time. They let themselves get weighed down by these ideas. And before they know it, they develop a negative emotional association with learning. It seems mentally painful.

The last time that they tried to learn a new concept, they were under a tremendous amount of stress and pressure. They don't want to go through that again. So if this is your attitude, don't be surprised if your brain sends you all sorts of negative signals when it comes time to learn a new concept.

This is going to be a problem because as a human being, you're going to have to learn new concepts every day. They may not be big, they might even be as small as a minor revision that you already know, still, you have to learn.

But if you have a negative emotional association with learning, you end up feeling intimidated. It feels like a chore. In fact, if you don't watch yourself, it might even feel like you're pulling teeth.

Considering this backdrop, it is no surprise that people burn out. They feel that they're juggling so many things at once that they end up snapping.

Now, by "snapping," I'm not saying that they experience some sort of psychotic break. I'm not saying they go crazy. Instead, they experience a cognitive break. In other words, they cannot learn.

Try as hard as they might, they just can't learn. And it's the most frustrating thing in the world. How can they? They've overloaded themselves.

If you're reading this book, you probably know exactly what I'm talking about. You've probably been here.

What is the solution? Take more learning breaks. Seriously. Just take a break.

When you do this, you get emotional release. Whatever concept you're trying to master no longer is hanging over you. It doesn't feel like some sort of giant with a big club about to smack you upside the head. This relieves all sorts of pressure, and this leads to stress detox.

Remember, the stress that you're feeling is not just in your head. It's registering in your physical body, thanks to the hormone cortisol. Your adrenaline system is also not being helped. So when you lift this intellectual weight off your shoulders, not only do you get a nice emotional release and an intellectual break, you also get a physical stress detox.

Just Give It a Rest

Seriously, just give it a rest. Stop consciously trying. When you give yourself time to take a break, take a break. Don't think about what you're reviewing or what you're studying. Give it a rest.

How do you do this? Well, I'm not saying that you should just blank out your mind. That's a bad idea. Instead, just fall back on what you already know.

Lawyers would call this "status quo ante." In other words, focus on your state of mind and state of knowledge prior to the stuff that you are trying to learn now. Fall back to it. This doesn't mean reformatting or wiping out your memory banks.

Once you have fallen back on what you already know, just focus on comfort. Allow yourself to be comfortable.

You'll Be Surprised at How Much You Retain

Believe it or not, when you fall back on what you already know after putting in the time to learn new concepts and just allowing yourself to relax, you're in for a shock.

When you don't put any pressure on yourself, you're actually freeing yourself up to repeat what you already know and whatever new stuff you're trying to pick up. This leads to an easier sense of mastery. I can't emphasize this enough.

Often times, our sense of mastery is what drags us down. We are so insecure that we're not learning fast enough or we're not learning in a deep enough way that we put too much emotional and intellectual pressure on ourselves. Guess what happens? Your sense of mastery starts to break down. You feel even more desperate. You feel even dumber.

Don't do that. Just vaporize the pressure. Just keep repeating stuff. When you do this, you get that sense of mastery. It feels more effortless.

And once this happens, you regain your sense of competence. A bulb lights up in your head, "I get this" or "I am getting this."

That sense of competence doesn't exist in a vacuum. The more you feel that, you gain greater confidence. And what happens?

This enables you to absorb more stuff through repetition. This leads to more mastery, which leads to a greater sense of competence, greater confidence, even more mastery, and on and on it goes. It's an upward spiral.

The reason why you're feeling stressed and pressured right now is because you may be caught in a downward spiral. The good news is, you can choose to reverse it by simply taking a break. Don't be afraid to take a break.

Here's the thing, though. You have to do it on purpose. You're not doing it out of frustration or desperation. When you do that, you're just focused on the relief and nothing else.

Take a programmed break. Just say, "Okay, at this point, I'm not going to think or talk about anything that I'm trying to learn. Instead, I'm just going to fall back on what I already know. I will allow myself to calm down." You'd be surprised as to how effective this is.

In a University of Texas 2014 study led by Dr. Alison Preston, the 35 adult participants were asked to memorize two sets of photographs in two separate tests. In between the tests, the study participants were asked to take some time off and just relax. They don't have to think about the photos. They can think about whatever they want.

When they were administered the second test, they were given brain scans. Interestingly enough, of the 35 adult participants who took the break, those who reflected on the first set of photos they saw were able to do better in the second test. What made this very interesting is that the improvement involved otherwise easy to miss minor details that overlapped among the two sets of photos.

This study suggests that when people are asked to relax, they are able to tie in the things that they already knew with absolutely novel information. This is how we embed or imprint new information. Just by taking a study break during the learning process, we can help the mind rest enough to get re-energized for such association.

The study also found that when people were daydreaming and let their minds wander, this exercise actually helped their brain retain more info as well as consolidate more info.

Now if you are reading this book for too long, go take a break and let your mind wander to strongly embed the information you just learned. I'll see you in the next chapter, when you come back.

Chapter 9: Make Learning Part of Who You Are

Has this ever happened to you? You are studying for a test, and it seems that regardless of what you eat, where you sleep, what you watch on TV, and what you play on your mobile device, it's all about the concepts you're trying to learn.

I remember a big test that I had to take and for three weeks, all I can think and talk about were the concepts being tested by that exam. Sure enough, I passed. But guess what happened? I can't for the life of me, remember even 10% of the stuff that I picked up during those three weeks.

I am hardly alone. Most people learn through information in, information out. How come? Well, we think that our minds can only hold so much, so to make space for new information, we have to clear out a lot of old ones. Once we have passed the test, got the promotion or job, or passed probation period, we then clear that stuff out for even more new information. It goes on and on.

Most people "learn" this way. "What's the point of learning concepts if you quickly forget them?' That's the question begging to be asked. The good news is it doesn't have to be this way. Another is "what's the point of learning concepts if they don't make learning other concepts easy?" Did you know that you can learn in such a way that it can lay the foundation for even more information? Instead of playing this mental reformat game with yourself, you can make space for even more information. How?

Incorporate whatever you learn into your identity

If you're able to do this, you're not just clearing out "hard drive space" in your brain. You're not going to be stuck with the familiar case of information in, information out. Instead, you are able to hang on to a lot of information, lock it deep inside your consciousness, and recall it when you need it.

Instead of this information taking up large chunks of your conscious memory, you can incorporate it into your "mental DNA". It doesn't take much space but when you need it, you're able to understand process setting and key concepts. You are able to recall this material right when you need it. It all boils down to incorporation.

Incorporate the things that you learn into your identity. Your identity is kind of like an information storage "deep freeze". In this, information is seriously compressed but rapidly extracted and recalled. Once you have used the information, you clear it out of your conscious memory but it's still locked in your mental deep freeze.

The key here is to incorporate the process of the content and the setting, "what is the context of this concept?", and then incorporate the key concepts, "what are the subcomponents of the concepts?".

How to make concepts you learned part of who you are

How exactly do you practice this "mental deep freeze"? First, mention it in your diary. I know this may seem pretty innocuous, even shallow and simple but it's effective. Mention it in your diary. When you do this, it jogs your memory. It also draws parameters. This protects you from false memories or memory corruption.

Believe it or not, memory corruption happens far more frequently than we are aware. Often times, two memories collide and we confuse them with each other. You're thinking of a memory and you are picking up stimuli and this somehow degrades your recall of your memory.

You should also mention concepts in your stories. For example, you're telling a story to your friends. Try to incorporate mnemonic parts or bits and pieces in to it. Understand this is not always doable, but if the opportunity presents itself, take it.

Incorporate jargons in your daily conversations. Again, this boils down to applicability. If it applies, for example, you're a law student or a lawyer and you're trying to remember subrogation or hearsay, incorporate bits and pieces in your conversation.

The same applies if you're a nurse, doctor or you work in the medical field. There's a lot of complicated jargon and hard to remember concepts there. Whatever the case may be, mention these concepts as part of your daily routine, but always keep a "hard copy" in the form of a diary entry.

This is the pristine or virgin version because this acts as a reference. Maybe you're telling stories all the time and you think you're incorporating all this but it turns out, you are using a corrupted version or a badly copied version. This happens. It's great when you have an uncorrupted version in your diary.

In 2004, the University of Regensburg in Germany, published a very famous study led by Bogdan Dreganski. Forty-five study participants were monitored by MRI machines to track how their brains changed or didn't change while they tried to learn to juggle things.

It turns out that when people are learning new complicated motions that involves eye coordination as well as dealing with a rapidly changing set of stimuli, the actual physical anatomy of the brain changes. In other words, when you're neurons start to make new connections because you learn something new, this is an actual physical change. This is not a change in the function of your brain but an actual change in the physical structure of your brain. This is gray matter change.

In addition to this shocking discovery, the researchers found that those who did the best in learning new tasks, incorporate this change in their lifestyle. Not only is it registered in the brain, but it's also registered in how people function. If you turn whatever it is you've learned into a part of you, it can enhance your performance and it can last a far longer time.

Chapter 10: How To Push Yourself & Sky-Rocket Your Learning Pace

Make no mistake, accelerated learning is all about flexing your intellectual muscles. Your brain is not just a mass of fatty tissues resting at the top of your spine. It is also an intellectual muscle. And just like any other muscle, it only grows both in strength, capacity, and size if you apply pressure to it. If you don't engage or challenge it, don't be surprised if your mental acuity starts to decline.

A lot of people think that if they don't challenge what they know or their ability to learn, that they'll just go on the same way like they did before. They assume that they would stay at the same level. That's not true. Just like with your physical muscles, they start to get weaker and weaker. They get softer until you are not able to do much at anything at all with them. The same applies to your brain. If you think that you can coast through life, you have another thing coming.

You have to challenge it. Not every once in a while, not once a month, but every single day. Seek to learn new concepts daily. This should not be hard, even if you just read the digital newspaper on your mobile device, you're sure to pick up a few new concepts every day. Read the financial section or even the entertainment section, sometimes they raise new concepts. Whatever the case may be, consciously seek to learn something new daily.

Now here's the trick. You have to switch from field to field. In other words, you have to vary your intellectual diet. For instance, if you like reading TMZ, which is an online gossip website, you can still engage your mind. But the problem is it reaches a certain status quo. You eventually reach a point when you're no longer challenging yourself.

By searching for an entertainment or gossip to financial news to political theory to art history to spiritual or religious material, you mix things up. You keep yourself on your toes. You don't settle into a routine.

Ideally, you should take on very complicated topics. What do I mean by this? Think and talk about things that are totally unfamiliar to you. Similarly, look at familiar concepts that are presented in a very challenging format. Maybe you're used to reading gossip in the form of a blog post or online diary complete with pictures. Well, it's a different experience when you consume that type of information in a form of a debate or social or lifestyle critics duking it out about the next Kanye West album or NBA commentators using all sorts of infographics and historical data to hash out their difference.

Whatever the case may be, even a change in format is enough to give you some level of cerebral challenging. You can also take on more complicated topics in the form of a challenging setting. For instance, you're in a crowded subway, people are talking all around you and you're not wearing headphones. You are focusing on a piece of information in front of you. This is an intellectual challenge because it pushes your ability to focus to the next level.

Finally, you can take the ultimate test and actively seek out information that has a very rough reputation. What do I mean by this? Well, this material is infamously hard to understand. You don't have to search far. For example, in the world of literature, you only need to read James Joyce's "Ulysses". Boy, is that a tough book to read.

You can also read stuff by Thomas Pynchon. There are many authors out there that present really interesting information and stories in a hard-to-follow and challenging way.

To take the ultimate test, you might want to consider philosophical authors. I wish every philosophy scholar wrote as clearly as Aristotle or even Plato. But they don't. If you really want to challenge yourself, read what I read in college. Michael Foucault. Maybe it's the fact that his scholarship was originally in French and was later translated to English that makes his materials challenging to say the least. Maybe it's just the way he presented the information.

For the ultimate challenge however, in the past 50 years, a few can even come close to the writings of Jacques Derrida. He is infamously complicated and hard to understand. In fact, he is one of the founding fathers of the modern Deconstructionist movement.

I'm raising all these with you, because you cannot let your intellectual muscles atrophy. You really can't. You have to challenge it. And the more difficult or unfamiliar the concepts you're trying to pick up, as well as the forms they take, the more you give your brain a workout.

Understand that this is not just a simple matter of volume. A lot of people tell me that they get a nice intellectual workout reading tons of texts. After all, this is one of the most basic college skills you would learn.

There are a lot of public intellectuals in the United States currently who say that college is a waste of time and money. They keep saying "what does it prepare you for anyway?". Try telling that to students who has to read hundreds of thousands of words every single week.

This is not just a simple matter of being able to process a lot of information, this also involves coming up with workable strategies to process and retain as much of that information as possible. This is a serious life skill. You don't necessarily have to go on to law school, an NBA or medical program to benefit from this. The fact that you're able to commit and practice some level of disciple to get this done and walk out of there with good grades, prepares you for a lot of challenges in life.

The bottom line is simple. Training your personal learning ability is like building your muscles. It takes commitment, focus, and discipline.

In a 2011 paper out of the University of Louisville, lead researcher Keith Lyle, reports that in his study of 24 experiment participants, those who were given a quiz regarding information they just learned tended to significantly outperform the other group which were not given quizzes. In other words, when you learn something new and challenge your absorption of that information through quizzes, you are more likely to retain that information.

When you challenge you ability to pick up information and retain it, in whatever form, you increase your performance. Make no mistake, your learning muscles are similar to your physical muscles. You are able to hang on to information better, as well as position yourself for better learning by constantly engaging your learning capabilities. You have to keep applying pressure to your learning muscles.

Conclusion

You are a learning machine. Do yourself a big favor and stop operating at a very low level. Don't think that once you have discovered to learn a certain way, that's all you need. Like I said in the introduction of this book, most people stop at the high school level, if not earlier.

Understand that you're carrying around some sort of intellectual wallet. Just like a physical wallet, it can only contain so much pieces of paper or business cards. But here is the good news. Your intellectual wallet, unlike your physical wallet, can be expanded tremendously. That's right, you can increase the amount of info your mind can hold.

Just as importantly, you can increase the value of the information your mind can hold. With this understanding, you would be able to turbo-charge your ability to learn and practice new information. Not only would this help you in your relationships and enable you to become a more persuasive person as well as enhancing your ability to explain things, it can also help you professionally.

As you probably already know, your labor market value turns solely on your skills. If you're picking up all sorts of skills whether online or offline, whether in a virtual environment or through traditional brick and mortar higher education institutions; you have to pick up stuff when you need it and at a really high level. This is how you leave everybody else behind. You can't do any of these.

If you think that you can only learn so much and that your best learning days are way behind you, even though you may be able to wrap your mind around the importance of learning, you have to operate with a sense of urgency.

If you think all this is something that would be "nice if it happened", you won't make much progress. You have to pursue and work on this. More importantly, you have to be passionate about it. Desire learning as much as you desire breathing. I wish you nothing but the greatest insight, knowledge, wisdom, and success.

DISCLAIMER

While all attempts have been made to verify the information provided in this publication, the author does not assume any responsibility for errors, omissions, or contrary interpretations of the subject matter herein.

The views expressed are those of the author alone and should not be taken as expert instruction or commands. The reader is responsible for his or her own actions.

The author makes no representations or warranties with respect to the accuracy or completeness of the contents of this work and specifically disclaims all warranties, including without limitation warranties of fitness for a particular purpose. No warranty may be created or extended by sales or promotional materials. The advice and recipes contained herein may not be suitable for everyone. This work is sold with the understanding that the author is not engaged in rendering medical, legal or other professional advice or services. If professional assistance is required, the services of a competent professional person should be sought. The author shall not be liable for damages arising here from. The fact that an individual, organization of website is referred to in this work as a citation and/or potential source of further information does not mean that the author endorses the information the individual, organization to website may provide or recommendations they/it may make. Further, readers should be aware that Internet websites listed in this work might have changed or disappeared between when this work was written and when it is read.

Adherence to all applicable laws and regulations, including international, federal, state, and local governing professional licensing, business practices, advertising, and all other aspects of doing business in any jurisdiction in the world is the sole responsibility of the purchaser or reader.